Does the
Washer
Really Eat The
Socks!

Table of Contents

DOES THE WASHER REALLY EAT THE SOCKS

Over the years, I have discovered that one of the big mysteries of the universe is this: Does the washing machine really eat all the socks? If so, how many and how often do they eat? I am assuming that feeding time comes whenever you put socks in the machine. If you are reading this book then I imagine you know exactly what I am talking about. Like me, you probably wonder where all the mates have gone for your children's socks, your husband socks, your own socks, just socks in general?

It seems the socks didn't like to stay together, especially the way my home was run. I often thought it must be the washing machine's fault. I wondered, how do they eat the socks and why do they like them? Which brands eat the most? Has there ever been a study done on washing machine sock-eating? Had GE or Whirlpool or Speed Queen or Amana ever checked this out? I concluded that some washers must be hungrier than others, because I know people who have a bushel basket full of mismatched socks.   And since the socks are

missing, it must be the washer. What else could

it be? I invite you to explore the answer with me

throughout this book, and hopefully have a

laugh or two along the way.

IN THE BEGINNING

Let's just say I haven't always been the world's best housekeeper. When my husband and I were first married and had no children, we had an opportunity to go away for a few days. The morning of our departure, we finished our breakfast of oatmeal, quickly packed our bags, and left, leaving the dirty dishes on the table with the leftover oatmeal in them.

Unfortunately, it was a hot and humid summer and we didn't have any air conditioning in our apartment. When we returned home, we had a surprise waiting for us: moldy oatmeal, one of my not-so-proud moments. I wouldn't consider moldy oatmeal healthy, but then again, where does penicillin come from?

Do you realize how hard it is to clean, scrub, or sandblast caked-on oatmeal. I've never enjoyed doing the dishes—at one point in my life I literally had every dish in the house dirty. At the time, we couldn't afford paper plates; besides I probably didn't think about using them anyway. There was stale milk in glasses and sticky residue on everything. Thank God for family. My sister, Joan, and sister-in-law Anna had pity on me and spent the better part of a day scraping, soaking, and scrubbing. Finally, with all three of us working, we reached the bottom of the dirty-dish pile. At least until the next meal. That was my usual routine at that time of my life.

Another problem—well, let's face it, I had many problems—was ironing. This was a biggie since the clothes would mildew because they would sit so long after I'd sprinkled them. This was before permanent press and steam irons where you just had to sprinkle your clothes with water and let them sit a few hours—*not days or weeks*—before you ironed.

There were unbalanced checkbooks, important missing papers, late payments due to lack of organization—plus who could find a stamp? I had cracked gravy in the refrigerator along with strange-looking things, which were sometimes green and scary. Maybe a good science project but not so much for leftovers! (FYI: cracked gravy is made by putting the leftover gravy uncovered way in the back of the refrigerator where you forget you have it. After a week or so, when it really dries out, it will crack in the middle.)

I typically stayed in my bathrobe until noon—a bathrobe that usually had jelly dripped on it from my toast as I watched television or talked on the phone to escape my messy house. Thank God we didn't have Skype or Face Time back then. I desperately wanted a way out of the mess but I didn't know how to get there. I couldn't afford a maid, and I figured burning the place down was illegal. But how could I continue to live like this? I had a sister and sisters-in-law, and friends who had children;

some of them even worked outside the home. Yet their houses didn't look like mine. Why couldn't I do whatever they did? I guess I never really asked, and I probably would not have listened anyway. They were kind enough to come help me clean every once in a while, and my house would look great—for about five to ten minutes. I wanted things to be different, but I just wasn't sure how or even if I could change.

I am convinced that disorganization breeds more and more disorganization. It continues to grow until you feel totally out of control. I know the reason most often given for disorganization is lack of discipline, and while I believe some of that is true, I believe the main reason for it is lack of knowledge. I needed to know *how* to clean it up and *how to* keep it that way. If you are reading this book, you are probably wondering the same thing. What do I do? *Where do I start and how do I continue this as a lifestyle?* I am going to try to answer these questions by sharing with you what I have learned and am still learning.

First, let me make it clear that not only is disorganization chaotic, it is expensive too. For example, I would regularly thaw out meat for dinner and later decide I didn't really want to cook it or didn't have time to prepare it after I'd spent all afternoon watching shows on television. Or I'd spend the time on the phone complaining to friends about my life. That resulted in hot dogs and macaroni and cheese or something like that for dinner many nights. At a later time—often when my husband wasn't around—I would throw out the meat once it met the right criteria—green, slimy, and smelly.

Unfortunately, that is not the only thing we wasted money on. Do you know how many unnecessary purchases you make when you don't know how many shampoos, conditioners, and lotions you have and where they are? We would buy cleaning supplies and all manner of things, and when we couldn't find them, we would just go out and buy more.

As I mentioned before, in my life before I got organized there were always dirty dishes. Most of the time, I didn't even clear off the table after dinner. I guess I put the food away, but I didn't clean up the dirty dishes. If someone came for coffee the next day (which in those days were a lot of mornings), I would just push the dirty dishes out of the way on the table to make room for their cup of coffee. I wonder now how I found a clean cup. In my mind, there never was a reason to clear up the night before because I was going to be perfect any day now! I always thought that one day I would get the house all organized and cleaned and then I would be perfect. The fact is, I took a journey from being in a mess all the time, to learning some old truths that are still the right thing to do. My house is now presentable 95 percent of the time.

***

The first house we bought needed work, so we started in the upstairs bedroom. I was so excited about it. The day finally arrived to start our wonderful project. The morning of the big day we began to strip the wallpaper off. To be helpful, my job was to clean up. I would grab large clusters of stripped-off wallpaper and go downstairs through the dining room and into the kitchen where I deposited my armfuls on the floor. Then, quick as a flash, I would go back upstairs and get another giant cluster of dead wallpaper and take it down and dump it on the kitchen floor—until at last, I had a couple of feet of very dead wallpaper all over my kitchen floor! It was about that time that my husband's cousin Tanya came knocking on the back door. As I waded through the deep pile and tried to pull open the door, the papers scraped on the floor and stuck to my shoes, as well as under the door, but I pulled and pulled and finally got the door open. I was very embarrassed and tried to explain, but how do you explain stupidity?

Looking back I think, why didn't I have a garbage bag upstairs to begin with and deal with it on the spot? That is a good question and the answer is, I didn't think like that at the time. It is one of the many, many things I have learned

along the way.

When my daughter Penny was little, I

learned another good lesson. One morning I

allowed her and her friend to go outside to play.

It was a beautiful sunny day, so I thought it

would be okay for her to go outside. I was still

in my shorter pajamas (back then I didn't look

too bad in them!). As I went to brush my teeth, I

thought I had better look out and see what the

girls were doing. Now, we lived close to a

railroad track and—yep, you guessed it—as I

looked out, there were the girls having such a

good time walking and pulling their little red wagon right toward the railroad tracks. I looked at myself in the bathroom mirror and thought, *Well, I can't go out like this. What am I going to do?* I saw my long coat in the closet and grabbed it. With toothpaste foaming from my mouth and a long coat on and my spanking stick, I ran out of the house yelling at my daughter to come back. Perhaps I forgot to mention that we lived in a town with cars that went by frequently. I'm sure I looked like a crazed woman in my long trench coat, foaming at the mouth on a hot day and spanking a little girl with a red wagon. It's a wonder the guys in

the white coats didn't come and put me away.

The thing I learned that day was, don't let your

children out of the house unless you are dressed

and your teeth are already brushed!

I don't think the girls ever went down by

the tracks again.

***

Since I always slept as long as I could, my

children would often get up before me. One day,

I thought I heard water running in the kitchen.

When I got to the doorway, I saw my sweet little

Penny Jo up on the sink with a big smile on her

face as she looked up at me. She thought she was really helping me. But the water had filled up the sink and was spilling over onto the floor. The reason the sink plugged was probably because it was full of potato peelings and other garbage from the night before. I yelled at her, when in reality it was my fault.

Being unorganized causes so much frustration in your life and in your family. When I think back to when I was raising kids, I'm reminded of how many times I yelled at them for the way their room looked or because they could not find their homework or the library book they had to have right then. When we are not doing our jobs well and training our children, we tend to get angry at ourselves for being so unorganized and then yell at them (at least that's what I did).

I was raised in a generation where it was very important to do the right thing; your word was your bond. If you told someone you were going to do something, you'd do it. Keeping your word is important. I am very thankful for my upbringing.

Throughout this book I hope to teach you some important lessons and how-to's of organization. This is the story of my journey, from moldy oatmeal to company-ready 95 percent of the time. The other 5 percent of the time? Just do what Phyllis Diller always said: "Keep some get well cards and put them up quickly and tell people you haven't been feeling well lately.

***

I remember vividly the day I finally decided to get organized. I had read a book a few days before about how to clean and organize your home and it gave me a huge desire to get my house organized, but I had yet to start. This particular day I was doing my normal thing—lying on the couch in my blue zip-up bathrobe watching television with lots of dirty dishes sitting in the kitchen, and a messy house—when a friend knocked at the door. I got up and made my usual excuses—I hadn't been feeling good, I was so busy with getting the kids off to school, I was planning to do a serious cleaning a little later—but that day was different. I was tired of being embarrassed and unmotivated. When she left I told myself this would never happen to me again, and so began my journey to organization and to find out once and for all if the washer

really did eat the socks.

PROCRASTINATION

I was born and raised in a family of eight
children, although we were not all at home at
once as there is an age difference of twenty-
three years between the oldest and youngest. My
dad was a farmer and also worked in a factory
every day. My mother helped on the farm and
raised the kids. I have many fond memories of
growing up and to this day we are a close
family. My mother was not at all what you
would call organized. She was clean and would
especially have clean floors, but to find what

you needed, you had to hunt for it—or do what my mom did, which was pray, and then she would find it. Mom was a talented person. She played the piano, which I think kept her sane. She also wrote the neighborhood news for the local paper for many years. I have many family stories and information in albums because of her writing.

And so, I grew up in a jumble of sorts. The laundry was just always in baskets in a bedroom we didn't use. When we needed something to wear we would dig through the baskets to find it. I don't remember that being a problem most of the time—after all, I made it to adulthood. I think because of being raised that way I have always pretty much kept up my laundry. I know laundry is a real problem for a great many people and we will talk about that later in the book. But I have always washed, folded, and put away my clothes pretty regularly because of my childhood. Now, the rest of the house and the dishes were another story.

After years of disorganization, I finally realized my biggest problem was procrastination, which means to postpone action: the art of putting things off. How many things in your life have you postponed? Why do we procrastinate? Why do we put off and put off things we *know* we need to do? I don't know the official answer to this question. All I know is what I do and how it makes me feel. In fact, the biggest thing I have procrastinated in is writing this book. Insecurity and many other things in my life kept me from writing for a long time.

There have been days when I had time to work on this—lots of days, as a matter of fact— and yet I would put it off. Procrastination is like a veil that covers your eyes and makes things cloudy. It is like a huge weight that you carry around knowing that you have things that need to be done, but the television, the chips and cookies are calling your name—and besides, there is always tomorrow. When there is that one thing that you know you need to do, your life becomes cloudy until you make an intentional decision to change and bite the bullet and get busy. Each time we postpone action it strengthens the procrastination in that area. Each time we choose to take action it makes us stronger in that area. Take a minute to consider in which area are you procrastinating.

If you were to have time off from work this week and someone asked you what you planned to do with that time, what would you say? You might respond, "Well, I am going to work around the house and get some things done." The problem with that is that it is so vague that you probably will go back to work from your time off without having really accomplished much at home. You have to plan your days. The Word of God says that we are to number our days (Psalm 90:12). What does that really mean? If you really don't care if you get anything done, then you will hit your mark. But if you truly want to accomplish some specific thing you must put a plan into action—what day, what time—and then discipline yourself to do it.

We are all capable of so much more in our lives. Whatever path God takes us on, we must stay on it and work. I understand that all these words are easy to say but are much harder to actually do.

Do you have big dreams? I think we all have dreams—some small and some really big. It is good to have dreams, but without a plan they will still just be dreams that never come true. My dream was to be organized and have a clean house. I just didn't know for sure where to start. I see so many talented people with lots of great ideas, but no real focus and plan. I think sometimes we think that what we want will magically happen, but that is not the way it works. I have also noticed that a lot of people are nice and giving, but unfocused. If you want a neat house and garage and everything in between, or if you want to paint the new *Mona Lisa* or write the great American novel, you must have a plan, and then work the plan. Since this book is written for the purpose of helping you organize your home and life, I will stick to this subject—besides I am not an artist and have not written the great American novel, so I will stick to what I do know. Our lives are not made by the dreams we dream, but by the choices we make!

"Our chances for success grow when we refuse to stop trying!" "Failing to plan is planning to fail!"

I have had these sayings taped above my computer to help me remember those truths. What is stopping you? When we have something we want to accomplish, what is it that is stopping us? I believe it's often fear. But 2

Timothy 1:7 tells us, *"God has not given us a spirit of fear, but of power and of love and of a sound mind"* (NKJV). Have you ever noticed that decisions never get easier tomorrow or next week? Are we willing to pay the price for waiting until we feel like doing something? Can we decide to do what it takes to propel us in the right direction, or will it just be wishes? Hebrews 11:6 says, *God is the "rewarder of those who diligently seek him."* Will we do it? Will we be intentional in seeking him and doing his will? In the same way, if you want to become organized or accomplish a project, you must be determined not to quit. We should never give up and we are never too young or too old to do what's been placed on our hearts.

We often think the easy way is to give up, but in reality it's very hard, because there is always guilt and regret and that is hard to live with.

Why do we sabotage ourselves? Why do we set ourselves up to fail? We have a tendency to put other things that need to be done ahead of our main goal, which allows us to excuse ourselves from not meeting our deadlines.

Like disorganization, procrastination is also expensive. When we postpone things like paying the bills or waiting until the sale is over or not getting paperwork done on time, we have to pay extra fees and lose out on a good deal. It is only by doing something that it will ever get finished. "Procrastination saps power, completion gives relief!" (Daily Bread). The answer to the problem of procrastination is to do it now. Make that phone call, pay that bill, fill out that paper the children need for school and put it in their backpack before it gets lost. Think of all the time we lose by not doing it when it needs to be done. The crazy thing is, so many things can be done in a very short time. Procrastinators always think it's going to take too long. But in reality, many tasks can be completed in a few minutes. I recommend you do what I did. Time yourself on some project you don't want to do—I think you will be amazed by how little time it will take. I have done that many times and I am always shocked by how little time it really takes—and by how much better I feel once it's done!

For a behavior to be classified as procrastination, it must be counterproductive,

needless, and delaying (procrastination/
Wikipedia).

Fear is first cousin to procrastination.
Everything I have read about procrastination
includes the mention of fear: fear of failure, fear
of success—fear. Consequently, procrastinators
often have anxiety, low sense of self-worth, and
are self-defeating.

Disorganization and procrastination go
hand in hand. One feeds the other. I know
people who have either quit or been fired from a
good job because they were so unorganized that
the weight became too heavy for them and they

didn't know how to get out of the mess they were in.

Though we might like to think it, children are not the only ones who put off the work they are supposed to do, and then when something fun comes along they can't enjoy it because they have to finish the work that was assigned to them. It happens to adults too. Most of us would love to have a magic wand to wave and everything would be done, but there is really only one way to

get something done, and that is simply to do it.

One of the ways I learned to get organized was to do the thing I dreaded to do the most. For me, that was doing dishes and cleaning up the kitchen. When I learned to do that first, everything else seemed so much easier. When the kitchen was cleaned the rest of the house seemed neater.

Even while writing this book, God reminded me that I could write for a time and then do the other things that needed to be done. When I did that I was at peace with myself.

Procrastination is not easy to overcome. But the good news is that the more often you make yourself do what you need to do, the easier it becomes. The price of procrastination is too high to continue in that habit. We have to do what we know needs to be done if we hope to fulfill our dreams and accomplish our goals.

We can become better homemakers, workers, and people by being responsible with our personal lives. Whatever your passion is, you need to be intentional and do the things that need to be done. One of my dreams was to have a house that was presentable most of the time, so when someone would drop by, I would be prepared. My dream now is to help you.

CLOSETS, CLOTHES AND LAUNDRY

Okay, so let's get started. The three areas people have the most trouble getting and keeping organized are clothes and laundry, paper (our office), and the kitchen. When we learn to deal with these three areas, the rest becomes much easier.

First we'll tackle the laundry and all the dirty clothes that pile up. Laundry needs to be done on a regular basis. Many people like to do their laundry a load or two a day. If that works better for you, go for it. I personally like to do mine two times a week unless I am washing rugs, sheets, blankets, or curtains, or have company visiting. I don't really like to do laundry, so if I do it twice a week, I can be done with it at least for a few days. Mondays and Thursdays are my laundry days and this works well for me. Regardless of how often you do laundry, the important thing to remember is that you fold and put the clean clothes away so they don't get wrinkled. I have seen people wait days to fold their clean laundry and by then the clothes are a wrinkled mess.

Of course, part of folding laundry are the dreaded king- or queen-size fitted sheets. I know many women are very neat with the way they fold fitted sheets; unfortunately, I was not born with that gene. I really tried with the sheets—I even watched YouTube videos of the correct way, and I practiced many times. This is what I finally did: I happened to find a really cool square basket at an estate sale, and after I got home I realized that my king-size sheets fit in that basket and the basket fit on the shelf of my closet. Now I do what I like to refer to as a neat wad of the fitted sheet. The flat sheet is folded a bit better, so if you put the wad inside the flat sheet and stuff it into the pretty basket, it looks pretty good! The main thing is to be able to find the clean sheets when it's time to change them. Later we will address the importance of having a place for everything, so you and your spouse and children know where things go and where to find them.

If you already have great big piles of laundry that have been lying on the floor for a long time, I suggest you wash it all and then carefully sort through it. I recommend using two clothes hampers. Put a large garbage bag in

each one and mark one trash and one for donate.
I do not believe it's a realistic plan to think,
Well, I will save these things for my future
garage sale. That kind of thinking is what got
you in this mess in the first place. Bless
someone else with the things you don't want
anymore.

Now back to sorting. If you don't wear an
item or the children have outgrown it *toss* it or
give it away. I know I am using four-letter
words that you may not like, but toss and give
are words you need to get used to if you really

want to live an organized life. Now, let's get those washers and dryers humming.

While we're letting the washer and dryer run, let me share a story that my niece Susie told me. She started her organization journey soon after I did. Here is her laundry story.

"Being a mom at a young age certainly had its challenges. At sixteen I had my first child. By nineteen I had two, and by thirty-one I had four great kids! Being organized always seemed to be the biggest challenge. If someone would stop by my house, I would run around and throw stuff in closets, drawers, anywhere to hide things before opening the door. I always really hoped no one would stop by because of how embarrassed I would be for anyone to see the mess!

One day I decided that *today* was going to be the day I did *all* the laundry. I always really wanted to be organized, so I loaded everything up that we had that was dirty. *Everything*. I had never had so many baskets of laundry. My goal was to get everything washed, dried, and put away in one day! I headed toward the only Laundromat in our little village. While driving through town I noticed people waving at me;

some were even flashing their lights at me. I thought it was a little odd but figured everyone was happy I was finally doing all this laundry, so I continued to the Laundromat. When I got out of the car, I saw what everyone was trying to tell me. There on the top of the car was a large box of Tide detergent. Somehow it made it all the way to the Laundromat without falling off! My life was crazy, and that was just one of the many things that was always happening to me. When I went inside, I filled up several washers. The owner of the business had pity on me and came over and helped me fold the laundry when it was all done. I was clearly in over my head with this project. I was there for hours. A lot of the laundry was mildewed from sitting so long in hampers. This is just one of the many times when disorganization caused a job that didn't need to be so overwhelming to be so because of the way I was doing it.

It was amazing to me to finally find a way to have everything in its place. An organizing system that worked! To be able to finally find the pencil sharpener when you needed it. Little things can take so much time, but when you know where things are, it makes so much more sense and makes life so much easier. Getting organized changed my life. I no longer fear company! I think many of us can relate to Susie's story.

Here is a question for you: How many sizes does it take to make a closet complete? Women especially have a tendency to have several sizes in our closets because we believe one of these days we are going to lose that weight and have that Bow flex body! Let me suggest that you move on and wait until you really need that new smaller size, and organize the clothes that fit now. Now, if you have the closet space or another closet that you use for off-season clothes, you can keep some of those things you really want to get into again, but let's be practical about it.

Alright, back to the sorting. You will need the hampers with the garbage bags again. You may also need two smaller paper bags—one marked Return and the other designated for items that go in a different place. The Return bag is for the books or DVDs or whatever else you find in your closet that belong to someone else that you forgot you had. The other bag is things like CDs or books or socks or whatever that need to go to another place. It's important

that you go through each box, pile, old purse,

whatever. You will be amazed at the things you

find. You will probably find things you have

been looking for a long time. It can be very

eye-opening. One lady that we helped organize

found a car fob that would have cost a lot to

replace and a gift card also. It does pay to go

through everything!

Next, clean off the shelves and take all the

piles off the floor. And of course, you need to

deal with all the shoes. You can purchase shoe

racks or just line them up neatly on the floor. I love to use baskets for organizing my shelves.

When the floor and the shelves are all wiped off and organized, you need to go through the hanging clothes. This is where a really good friend can be helpful. You need to ask if they think certain items look good on you. A really good friend will tell you the honest truth! Toss anything that is in poor condition, and donate clothing that you don't love or that your friend can honestly tell you doesn't flatter you. When you return the clothes you're keeping back to the closet, here are a few tips. I use all the same color hangers. It makes the finished closet look so much nicer. I tried using different colors for each person but that became a nightmare, so I just use white for everyone. I hang like things together—tops, sweaters, slacks, dresses. I also put like colors together in the groups, which can help you to see new outfits emerging. You might realize a shirt would look good with a certain pair of slacks, and so on. It really does make a difference. Keep your seasonal clothes in the back of the closet unless you have an extra closet you can use. This makes changing seasons much easier. Seasonal shoes can be put in shoe boxes or you can buy plastic ones that work well.

When we moved into our current house, the closets each had one shelf. I noticed how much space above the shelf was wasted and so my husband put another shelf above the original in all the closets. That has helped me so much over the years. Take a closer look at your spaces and rethink some of the ways you are currently doing things, and maybe you too can find more room. Remember, though: found room is not an excuse to keep more stuff that you really don't need, but it sure helps with the things you do keep.

***

Now that your closet is done it should be so much easier to put the laundry away. All the closets need this treatment, so enlist the help of your children and husband, especially when you are doing their closets. I know it seems overwhelming now, but even tackling one or two a week as time allows will have you finishing the job before you know it.

Just remember that as you put the clothes back in the organized spaces, always put them back where they belong. There is a temptation to hang or toss them anywhere, and you have to fight this easy way out and make yourself put them back where they belong. I call this the disorganized gene (also called the "just throw it now, and fix it later" gene). That is why we have to retrain and retrain. I still fight this at times.

Now that the closets are done, it's time to do the same to all the dressers. You know the drill: Does it fit? Do I love it? And so on. When you come across anything that is not clothes in the dressers (like pizza crust, apple cores, papers, buttons, twist ties, and pictures), if it's not trash, set it aside to go through later, after you're done sorting clothes. Wipe out the drawers and put back just the items that should be in that drawer. I use little plastic baskets for underwear and socks. When the kids were little, that helped greatly. It was much easier for them to put items in the right place, and that way the drawers stayed organized and it took less time to clean up, and time is what we all need.

PAPERS, PAPERS, PAPERS

Papers, bills, coupons, notes, junk mail advertisements. We all have it and it must be tamed! The first thing you need to do is get in the habit of dealing with mail immediately when it comes in. I have had people tell me they don't even open their mail, let alone know where they are financially. Start opening your mail over a shredder and or wastebasket. If you don't have a shredder, have scissors on hand. I usually just cut it in half when it's junk mail. If it includes important information that should be kept private, use the shredder. As you get into the habit of dealing with mail as it comes in, you will notice how freeing it is to not be surrounded by stacks and stacks of papers.

For the mail I keep, I use a plastic three-drawer system. The top drawer is for the incoming bills so they are handy when I sit down to pay them. The bottom drawer is for receipts after they have been paid. I mark them with the date I paid them and the check number. The middle drawer is used for a checkbook and a few important papers that I don't need as often.

When the bottom drawer is full, I empty it and put those things in their files in the regular file cabinet. You may prefer to skip the drawers and file in the regular file cabinet as you do your bills. As long as you actually do it, that might be the system for you! For myself, I prefer to use the plastic drawers. As with any problem, you have to solve it with what realistically works for your life.

We have a large four-drawer cabinet and I really only need the top drawer for all the folders that pertain to our household bills and receipts. I have a folder for medical bills, household receipts, insurance, birth certificates, our will, credit cards, and so on. Your life is different from mine, and so your files will be different as well. If you don't have a file cabinet you can use a cardboard box or one of those plastic crates. Use your imagination. Just make sure that whatever system you choose, it's a system you'll use. When we buy a new appliance I keep the instructions and I have them in binders. I always mark the date we bought it on the booklet of each item. I know now with the internet you may not need them, but I do use mine from time to time. It's your decision whether you keep them or not. You will need to go through them from time to time to toss the ones that you no longer need, like the coffee pot that quit working or the DVD player you sold at the garage sale.

I have my bills listed in a columnar pad; it's fifty sheets and it's 11 by 8 1/2 inches. I mark out three months at a time and list all the bills, and then I mark them paid as I go. You need to always look at your bills and make sure it is correct. Don't be intimidated to call the company and ask questions if something doesn't seem right. Any time I have called about an account, most companies will work with me and adjust it if need be. I highly recommend that you speak politely and they will often help you work the problem out.

Checkbooks need to be balanced on a regular schedule.

When I first got organized, I decided to balance my checkbook. I had cancelled checks everywhere and bank statements stacked up on every available spot and I was very confused. I called the bank and they asked me when I had last balanced my checkbook. I told them about seventeen years ago. It was very quiet at the other end of the line. They finally replied that I probably still had checks out and so on. I knew I had subtracted all the checks, but we were not understanding each other at all. I later decided to have a friend help me.

I guess my husband had balanced once in a while, and I was glad we were not in jail for writing bad checks. Now, of course, I bank online and it is awesome. I balance at least a couple times a week and it's so easy to do.

Your paper trail life will be so much easier after this initial stage. It won't take you seventeen years to balance your checkbook.

Although I know some people who do not write down their debits and subtract them regularly, I recommend you do this, even if online, so that you can keep up with where you are financially. Just keep in mind that a lot of times things don't hit instantly but you still need to consider that money spent. You also need to keep your credit cards and debit cards up to date. When you get a new one, be sure to cut up or shred your old one.

What about magazines? Have you ever noticed that magazine subscriptions constantly send renewal bills?I suggest that if you subscribe to them, use a 3x5 card and write down when you bought them and when they are due again so you have the documentation as to what and when you paid. You always need to date this information. A lot of money is wasted when we don't keep track.

As easy as it is to avoid the topic or forget its importance, it is so vital to have your affairs in order. Everyone needs a will and instructions of what to do in case of death. We have a red file in the front of the office file cabinet that all our children know about in case of our deaths. We have listed our bills and checking and saving accounts, insurance, and other important information, and we update that from time to time.

We also have our wills and I have explained it all to them. As much as we'd like to live until very old age, death can come very unexpectedly, and it's important to leave our family prepared and informed.

My nephew and his wife had two sets of twins, which was a miracle, since my niece had had a kidney transplant and had been told she could not have any children. And then, two sets of twins.

My nephew died very suddenly, while his children were still young adults. My niece (his wife) knew about the insurance and what to do. Unfortunately, she never told the children any of their business, and the children never asked, assuming their mom would be around a long time. Sadly, she also died unexpectedly.

Their children were all only in their twenties. While talking to some of them later, I asked what they wished they had known? One of the children said if they had known about the insurance and other important things it would have helped greatly. It took them eight months to get the life insurance collected.

When I asked how they figured out what to do, they said they went through box after box of old pay stubs, cancelled checks, and so on. They did not have a will so they contacted an attorney, and the funeral home owner also helped them. They made multiple calls to businesses and banks to see what accounts were still open.

I also asked what they learned from all of this. Number one, everyone should have a will. It's important to talk openly and make a plan. One of the children said his parents didn't throw anything away before or after their father had died. One of the sons told me he wished they had sat down as a family and made a plan before all this happened.

Another frustration for the children was that they didn't have phone numbers for some of the relatives to notify the family and friends. Contact names and phone numbers for the family and close friends plus the business people they will have to deal with should be in a place that the family is aware of.

So we've covered the importance of financial records and documents. But what about other paper? There are many things that fit into the paper category, like pictures, special cards, letters, and more. I suggest that while organizing the main part of your home, put all the pictures and letters and cards in a large tub or tubs and wait until you have the rest of the organizing done. You will enjoy them more and make better decisions later. The main thing is to leave no stone unturned when organizing.

I had an old trunk that was really full of cards, letters, high school keepsakes, and even some grade school things. It took me two days of reading, tossing, and keeping—and a few tears—but now I have just the things that really mean something to me—and that will probably be a great fire starter for the kids when we are gone!

One suggestion I have is to get a CD of pictures whenever you get them developed. It is worth the extra money so you can get copies or larger prints one day if you want to. If your phone camera is too full, get a CD to develop at a later time, like when you are done organizing and are fully in control of all your other stuff. There are also great online storage sites for pictures. You can upload images straight to certain websites and they'll print and mail them to you. One of the things I have done is make a scrapbook for each child when they are fifty (I was only 4 when I had my last child). I have one more to go but I keep a disc of all the pictures and give the pictures to them. That way I don't have to deal with as many pictures. In the year 2000, I started to scrapbook family pictures. As I've gotten older, I take fewer pictures because I know I have to deal with them.

Photos aren't the only sentimental paper we have to deal with. Magazines, letters, cards from special people… I know I have to deal with them, so only the really good and important ones are kept.

For the children's birthday cards, report cards, and things they've created, I bought an old-fashioned scrapbook and put all their paperwork in that. Of course, some things can be tossed. I took all the things I wanted to keep for them and filled a scrapbook for each child. Then when they left home I gave it to them (yes, they do leave home eventually). That way I was able to save things, but it was out of my house.

***

During this time of organizing, you will need to keep up with certain daily chores. Don't let the rest of the house suffer while you're focused on organizing paper and clothes. Make your bed every day as soon as you get up, even if the rest of the room is in shambles. You need this habit, because this will encourage you to continue on. Do your dishes every day, or have your husband or children do them. Just make sure you do them and put them away. The rest of the kitchen may be a mess but this will make a huge difference in your life. You also need to clean the stool and sink every week in the bathroom. And don't forget your plan for laundry—at least once a week, folded and put away, even if you haven't designated a place for all the clothes yet. These are important habits to establish.

Doing this will keep order while you are getting rid of all the stuff you don't need. This sounds like a lot of work but it's the habits that will propel you to the organized home you desire.

KITCHEN

The kitchen can be very overwhelming, but it doesn't have to be. If you take it one step at a time, even the most disorganized kitchen can be managed. When you get to the kitchen, the first thing you want to do is to wash all your dirty dishes and put them away wherever you can fit them. Clean off the counter and continue the same routine—throw away, put away—and then wash off the counter so you have some space to work. Start at one end of the cupboards and work your way around the room. Once again, use your two containers for items that are garbage and to donate.

Each time you open a cupboard think about what you have and what you actually use. How many mixing bowls do you really need? How many slow cookers, cookie sheets, serving spoons do you need and use? I have been in homes that have so many plastic containers in the cupboards that they fall out all over the floor every time you open the door. I'm not sure how many leftovers a person can have, but I think if you need that many containers, you have way too many leftovers.

One challenge of plastic containers is tracking down the lid that fits the container. I bought a set that fits nicely in the cupboard and the right lids are next to them. Also my granddaughter Sarah bought me a much nicer set with the correct lids . Items like this are the answer to some of the problems that cause so much frustration.

As with any space, you must take into consideration the size of your kitchen and how many cupboards you have. I have a very small kitchen, and when we put in new cupboards, we decided to go with ceiling-height cupboards to have more storage space. The dishes I use less often or for Christmas can be stored in the high cupboards. The down side of this is, as I grow older, I notice that the shelves seem to get higher. I do have a small stepladder but my best answer is my great-granddaughter, Ruthie. She gets on the counter and reaches what I need and she loves it.

It is very freeing to get rid of the things you don't need or use, particularly in the kitchen. Be sure and wash out the shelves as you empty them, and put back only the things you really need or love. For my pantry I bought the tiered shelves for canned goods, which helps in a small space. As you clean out your food pantry and cupboards, be sure to check dates on labels and get rid of things that are outdated. You may find some things you forgot you bought.

Kitchen drawers can become messy quickly, even after you have them all organized and clean. I use small baskets–you can get them in all sizes at the dollar store or wherever you shop. It is much easier to find the measuring spoons or other small items when they are sorted into smaller baskets instead of tossed into one big cluttered drawer. In my larger drawers I use the plastic silverware dividers; they work great for larger items and can be cleaned quickly. I also keep a crock conveniently by the stove for large spoons, spatulas, and so on, so when I am cooking I can easily reach what I need. There are so many wonderful ideas out there, but don't get sidetracked by endlessly researching all the ideas. Instead, choose one that best suits your needs and habits and try it out. You may discover a simple idea that transforms your kitchen organization!

After you've finished organizing the important kitchen items, you can spend some time decorating. If you have some cute shelves in the kitchen, wash them off and make sure the knick-knacks or whatever you want to keep are clean. In one of the houses we lived in before I got organized, we had this cute country-style shelf above the stove. I kept seasonings on it and a few cute knick-knacks, and when it was clean it was really cute. But it was also a handy place to toss items. One day I made a batch of old-fashioned chocolate fudge. My brother-in-law Roger came over and I offered him a big piece of fudge. When he bit into it there was a *nail* in the fudge! Thank goodness he was okay, but I was so embarrassed! Later I looked, and sure enough there were some nails on the shelf above the stove and one had fallen into the fudge. Lesson learned: clean off the shelf and don't put random junk on it.

One job that often gets ignored is the refrigerator; however, it's important to keep it cleaned out and organized. No one wants a sticky mess or disgusting mold on the fridge shelves, and if it's not organized, it's easy to overlook food that you have, which means it doesn't get eaten before it goes bad or you purchase items you already have.

Most refrigerators have a veggie drawer and meat drawer, which is helpful for organizing. I use some small baskets for boiled eggs so they are easy to access. I also take the wrapped sticks of butter out of the box when I put them in the refrigerator so it's easier to grab a stick as I need it. I try to keep like things together, like the mustard and ketchup and pickles. Again, organize in a way that works best for you. It's helpful to get into a routine of tossing the "dead stuff" weekly and wiping down the refrigerator. Every three months or so, you need to clean it by pulling out all the shelves and drawers and washing everything inside.

One of the scariest places in the kitchen besides the refrigerator is under the sink. It's always so dark, and things you have forgotten about live under there. The first thing to do is remove everything and wash it out. I put contact paper in mine and it looks so much better. Examine each item and determine whether you need it or use it. There are often many items under the sink that can be pitched into the trash can. Over the years, I have tried many techniques to make this space look nice; some have worked and some have not. Remember, my kitchen is small and so my space is limited. Like most people, I also have large pipes running through my under-sink cabinets. I've discovered that having a couple of bigger baskets that fit under the sink keep cleaning supplies organized and can be pulled out easily. I store the supplies that I use more often in the front, like the dish soap and the dishwasher detergent. Although I buy my dishwasher detergent in a large size, I keep that in the basement and fill a smaller container to put under the sink with the lid off so I can just reach in and put the soap into the washer.

After some experimenting, you will find the best way to organize your space to make it work well for you and your family. This is really all about making your life simpler and your home tidy. Another tip that has proved helpful to me is to completely remove the opening of boxes for items like sandwich bags and garbage bags so I can just reach in and grab what I need.

Keep in mind that organizing your kitchen could take a few days or a few weeks depending on how much time you have each day to deal with it and how large your space is. Remember that as you get each cupboard organized, keep it that way! An organized kitchen will make your home feel less chaotic and meal prep more efficient.

BATHROOMS AND BEYOND

Anyone who has seen a dirty, cluttered bathroom knows how important it is to keep bathrooms clean and organized. Even if you're like me, with only small bathrooms, you can organize them to fit your needs and make even a small space work for you.

First of all, I always keep a couple of rolls of paper on the back of the stool in a cute container and extra toilet paper under the sink so that anyone can change the roll when needed.

If you have children at home, they can do this as well; it's not rocket science to change a roll of toilet paper. (You may need to remind your husband of that as well.) I have a shelf on the inside of the door under the sink that I keep the bathroom and glass cleaners . This makes it easy to do a quick cleanup when it needs it. I keep toothpaste and floss in one of two drawers, and I have the toothbrushes in a holder on the counter. In the other drawer I keep things organized with smaller containers. Along with a curling iron, I have two small baskets to keep picks and combs and some face cream. My makeup bag sits in the drawer and I can conveniently reach in and grab it to quickly do my makeup. All these little things help to make life easier by keeping items at my fingertips. In the medicine cabinet I keep Band-Aids, Tylenol, and other items. There are a few other designated spots for things like shaving cream and razors. Keep in mind, you will want to put like items together. It is good to go through these from time to time and get rid of things you no longer need.

We keep bath towels in the hall closet, where they are folded and placed on the closet shelf for easy access. I have a smaller basket where I keep the washcloths. I also have a basket in the closet for all the vitamins and medicine, which makes it easy to fill our weekly pill containers. Remember, if you have young children in the home you will need to put medications out of reach. I use other baskets in that closet for extra shampoo, creams, first aid, and other things that I don't have room for in the bathroom. My advice when it comes to toiletries is to only buy things you'll actually use. The bathroom needs to be kept as tidy as possible. We will talk about the cleaning part later on.

For now, keep in mind that the more organized you are with each room and the more you can get rid of, the easier your life will be.

***

Let's move away from the bathroom and on to the living room and family room. When dealing with these rooms, I think it's easiest to start at the doorway and work your way around. Don't forget your two hampers with trash and donate bags, and perhaps the smaller bag for all those things you'll find that belong elsewhere.

Go through each cupboard, end table, coffee table, and shelf; get rid of all you can and arrange the things you are keeping in a neater way. Wipe off shelves furniture so that part is clean and neat. Then continue to go through the house and do this with all the rest of your rooms. Get the family involved and you will be amazed how efficiently you can work and many things you will find that you thought were lost forever. I realize that this all takes time and effort, but anything worth doing is going to take time and effort. Being disciplined is never easy, but it is essential to achieve your goals.

***

When I first started my organization journey, we lived in a home with a Michigan basement—that means it had the furnace in it and a stone wall and cement floor and it wasn't very big. This is the kind of basement where if a tornado came through, you might just take your chances upstairs because you really didn't want to hide from the storm down there. As I was organizing, I also cleaned out that basement so that I knew what was down there and where things were. Since I had done some canning at that time, I had a clean place to put my jars. I believe you need to organize every room—including the often forgotten attics, basements, and garages. You never know what items you'll find that you thought were lost.

If you work, whether outside of the home or from home, it will take you longer to accomplish this job. But with determination and perseverance, you can do it! Spend evenings or weekends going through a little bit at a time. Enlist the help of a friend who can support you as you sort through things, and then offer to help her organize her space. Just don't take your friend's discarded stuff home with you—you don't need it either!

All the small decisions about what you decide not to do, or the things you decide to do, have a big impact on the final outcome of your day. One of the most difficult things to learn is self-discipline—making yourself do something that you don't want to do.

Proverbs 27:23 says "*Be diligent to know the state of your flocks, and attend to your herds.*" I believe we can use this verse for our homes. Although I am pretty sure most of you reading this would not have any physical herds or flocks, I am sure many of us have more stuff than we will ever be able to use before it is no longer useable. I have seen houses that are kept up and presentable upon entering. The dishes are done and the laundry is finished and the floors are swept, but underneath the walls are closing in. The cabinets are stuffed with shampoo, lotions of all kinds, soaps, and more. People keep buying and buying and yet don't know what they have. Think of all the money that could be saved by knowing the "state of your flocks." Think of all the people you could bless by clearing out and cleaning out and giving all the extra things away. I am not against having extra supplies on hand, but I think you understand the difference. Remember: nothing will change until the excuses go!

I often hear people say, "I have to clean my house." Like, every day. I don't believe you have to clean your house every day. When you are organized and put things back where they belong, it will always look neat. Of course, you do have to clean the house regularly, but not every day. We will talk about cleaning schedules in a later chapter. The main thing to remember is how to have a household that is run with some semblance of order. You will not be perfect. The main thing is the organization underneath. If your drawers and closets and cupboards are in some sense of order, you can find things when you need them. Think of the arguments and frustration that could be avoided by just knowing where things are. You don't have to have a perfectly clean house all the time—that's impossible unless you have a full-time maid—but you can keep the laundry up and the dishes done and the bills paid on time with some basic home management. And that won't happen unless you make it a priority.

What is a priority? It is "the quality or state of coming before another in time, importance, or rank. Order of preference based on urgency or importance, a preferential rating that allocates rights to goods and services in limited supply (in time of war top priority is given to military requirements)." Getting organized is a type of war! It is war on clutter and stuff! So you must give it top priority in your life. This means that organizing becomes important to you in order to meet your goals in life. It is so easy to get sidetracked by something other than the main priority. It is human nature.

Remember, even not deciding is a decision. The next time you find yourself stuck, tell yourself, "I am going to only do this one area and then I will leave it for now." Most of the time you will continue on when you see it's not as difficult as you thought and it looks so much better than before. One of the things I have learned is to do the worst job first. By now you probably know that means I start with my dishes. Then the rest of the jobs don't seem so bad. In fact, I've even put a sign up in my office that says, "Do your dailies first and the cloud will go away." When I'm foggy and I really don't want to do anything, such as make the bed, I do the dishes and this cloud of indecision goes away. It has actually really helped me.

I want to share a story from my niece Susie about struggling to do something that needs to be done, but not wanting to do it.

"When I was running daily, there were days when I wasn't very excited about putting my jogging clothes on and going for a run. To motivate myself I would tell myself, "I am not running today, but I think I will just get my running clothes on." I would continue to tell myself, "I am not running today but I think I will get my running shoes on" and then, "I am not running today but I think I will just step outside for a few minutes." And finally, when I was outside, I was all ready to run. Running at that point didn't seem hard at all."

This may seems like a silly or simple way to motivate yourself, but it just might work for you when you're struggling to do the dishes or whatever you are dreading that you know needs to be done.

If you look at anything you have accomplished in your life, you've had to overcome days when you didn't feel like doing it but you kept pressing on day after day.

Sometimes you did only a little at a time and

some days more, but you kept on keeping on

and that is what causes success. I came across

the following saying one time and wrote it down

and put it where I could see it often: Do it—do it

because it's right, and then do it right (Ken

Copeland ministry.)

We have many things we want to

accomplish in our lives but we must determine

which ones are the main things for us to focus

on. If you are like a lot of creative people, you

want to do more than you realistically can do.

Don't fall into a fog because you get stuck not knowing what to do. Think through things before you get distracted and decide to try some new hobby. Stay focused on getting the organization done and then think of how much easier your hobbies will be.

For instance, I wanted to learn how to do the afghan stitch in my crocheting. I made one mitten and I never finished the other one. I guess I was hoping to find a one-handed person that needed one mitten and liked the color red. Well, I never did, and one of the happiest times of organization was the day I organized that basket of crochet items and I threw that mitten away. I knew I wasn't ever going to finish that project. It was very freeing. Unfinished things have a way of hanging over your head. Make decisions you need to make and go with it, even when other people think you should do it differently. Find your level of organization that you can live with.

TIME MANAGEMENT

Not only do we need to organize our home, but we need to organize our time. What does this mean and how do we manage it? Webster's dictionary defines *time* as: 1: to arrange or set the time of: schedule 2: to set the tempo, speed, or duration of 3: to cause to keep time with something (timed his steps to the music) 4: to determine or record the time, duration or rate of (timed the race).

There are so many sayings about time: Waste of time. Be on time. Time clock. Family time. Alone time. Time with God. Part Time. Time flies. Beat the clock. Time is precious. Time and time again. Time heals all wounds.

There are lots of thoughts about time. If you could put time in a bottle, like the song says, what would you do with it? We all have the same amount of time in each day. Rich or poor, old or young, educated or not. My mother-in-law, Lorene, often said, "Time waits for no man," and this is so true.

When we think about time management, it just makes sense that you can get more done in less time if you are organized. Being a good manager of your time is the only way to meet the goals in your life. We must learn to set realistic goals and plan effectively. How much time do you spend on social media, talking on the phone, texting, or watching your favorite television shows? When I first began to get organized, I started to time myself on different jobs to see how long it took. It was amazing to me how little time it usually took to get something done. How long does it take to make the bed? Most people can do it in less than three minutes. However, they will avoid doing it each day because it's too big of a job. Try timing yourself while you do tasks and you will be surprised at how fast some things can be done— and what a major difference it makes in the room and your attitude.

We all have the same amount of time in each day. Do you spend your time day dreaming about the goals you want to fulfill? Do you know where you need to start to achieve your goals? Organization in any area of our dreams is of utmost importance. Our time is the only time we have.

Again, I believe one of the best ways to manage your time is to really start timing yourself on some projects. Try to see if there is a faster or better way to do a job. Can you delegate some parts? Really look at what you do and why. Are the things you're doing helping you achieve your goals? There are many things we do without thinking about them and maybe you don't need some of those things in your life right now.

There are three types of people in the world: those who don't know what is happening, those who watch what is happening, and those who make things happen. Which one do you want to be?

If I had to declare a bottom line for this book it would be "a place for everything and everything in its place." If you have children (or even if you don't!), I recommend the book Mr. Cook's Spatula by Larry Green. It teaches kids the importance of the lesson "a place for everything and everything in its place."

THE PLAN

The first thing I learned to do before I had started any organizing or cleaning was to get up at least fifteen to thirty minutes before the majority of the household. I encourage you to do the same. Take this time to jump in the shower and get dressed and brush your teeth and comb your hair. I also do what I call "fluff." I put on a bit of makeup and it makes me look and feel better. Then I am ready for my day. This is a huge step in getting started organizing and cleaning.

Most studies show that it takes six weeks to establish a habit. I challenge you to try this morning routine for six weeks and see if it changes your life. Even now that my children are grown and we are retired, I still get up early and take my shower, spend time with my devotion and Bible reading, and then get ready for the day. Your stage of life may require you to do this morning routine a little different, but I still believe it is very important.

***

Now that you have the house organized underneath, and are keeping it as neat as possible, the next thing is to deep-clean the whole house. Keep in mind that during the underneath cleaning, you'll still need to keep up with the laundry and what I refer to as the dailies: making the bed, doing the dishes, taking care of the garbage, putting things back where they belong, and training the rest of the family to do these things. It's a lot of work but you need to know that with this plan you will not have to do it all at once.

I've learned that it's helpful to have a schedule for your days and weeks. You may feel overwhelmed, but planning works. If you work outside the home and have other responsibilities, you will need to make it flexible. This is a guide to help you accomplish your goal.

Sample Schedule

Monday: Do laundry and weekly cleaning

Tuesday: Work on some deep cleaning

Wednesday: Desk work, pay bills, other paperwork

Thursday: Laundry / work on organizing

Friday: Grocery shopping /errands

Saturday: Children

Sunday: Church/ family day

I realize this is may be unrealistic for

those who also work outside the home. You will

need to personalize this to fit your life.

This is simply a guide to help you set a schedule for yourself. It's amazing how much just sitting down and putting pen to paper will help you. Look at what days you have off and what can be delegated to others in your household. Look at your finances and determine whether you can hire some help if needed.

Remember, with a disciplined routine, after six weeks you will have established habits that will encourage you and your family.

Alright, let's move on. The next thing that needs to be done is the deep cleaning. I have provided sample lists for each room for you to incorporate into your schedule. After looking at the lists and the time periods, you will need to have a written or typed list that you can date when you finish a job and note when it should be repeated. I highly recommend Google calendar, as you can set it to repeat as needed. If you don't use a computer you could set up a notebook with the lists and check them off when they are done and add in the date they need to be repeated. You may want to just use a regular calendar that you fill in. You can do this by the month or by seasons—whatever works for you and your family.

To get you started, I have created the following list by room; you will have to make your own list for rooms I may not have included. Next to each task, I will use the following code: W for Weekly, M for Monthly, D for Daily, EOD for Every Other Day, S for seasonal, and Y for yearly.

This plan is the tool for organizing your home and life. Make additions or deletions as necessary. Remember, it should reflect your lifestyle. Also, the frequency that I have may not suit you, and that's okay. Do what works best for your family. Most of the monthly tasks

could possibly be done seasonally. And let's
face it—if you just did all this once a year it
would probably be better than what some people
do now.

KITCHEN

Wash Dishes (fill dishwasher)	D
Scour Sink	W
Wipe off counters, stove, etc.	D
Sweep Floor	D
Shake Rugs	D
Mop Floor	W

STOVE

Scour Drip pans   EOD

Clean knobs and outside   W

Clean oven   E3M

Pull out stove and Clean under   1 to 2 x Y

REFRIGERATOR

Toss dead things and wipe out

W

Take all shelves out and wash them and inside   E3M

Wash all outside and Top   E3M

Pull out and clean underneath   1 to 2 x Y

Clean out drip pan   E3M

CUPBOARDS AND DRAWERS

Empty and wash shelves and drawers   Y

Straighten cupboards and shelves   W

Wash Windows inside and out   2 x Y

Spot wash windows   W

Dump dead things out of cupboards   M

Wash canisters off   W

Empty canisters and wash inside and out 2 x Y

Wash Knick-knacks   2 x Y

Wash Woodwork   2 x Y

Wash and press curtains   1 x Y

Clean toaster, can opener, etc.   W

Empty waste basket and wipe out   W

Set Garbage out for pickup	W
Sweep Cobwebs	M
Clean microwave	W
Wash potholders	EOM
Clean coffee Pot	E3M or as needed

BATHROOMS

Wipe off counter sink and toilet	D
Wash mirror	D
Clean Tub	W
Clean Sink	W
Clean toilet	W
Clean Shower stall	M
Wash shower Curtain	E3M
Wash rugs	EOW
Spot wash window	W
Wash Windows inside and out	2 x Y
Wash Curtains and press	2 x Y
Sweep and mop	W

Straighten cupboards, drawers	M
Clean and Organize	2 x Y
Spot wash woodwork	W
Wash Woodwork	2 x Y
Sweep Cobwebs	EOM
Wash light fixtures	2 x Y

BEDROOMS

Make Bed	D
Change Sheets	EOW
Wash all bedding	2 x Y
Sweep/Vacuum	W
Dust Furniture	W
Dust Pictures	EOW
Clean and Organize closets	2 x Y
Clean and organize Drawers	2 x Y
Straighten closets /drawers	W
Wash Mirrors	EOW
Sweep Cobwebs	M
Move and Clean Under Furniture	2 x Y
Wash Curtains	Y

*Remember, this list applies to each bedroom

LIVING ROOM/ FAMILY ROOM/OTHER

Pick up and put things away	D
Sweep/Vacuum	W
Shampoo Carpet	Y
Dust Furniture	W
Wash windows	Y
Spot wash Windows	M
Wash Knick-knacks	2 x Y
Curtains/Drapes	Y
Move furniture and sweep under and out	E3M
Clean light Fixtures	2 x Y
Sweep Cobwebs	M
Clean and Organize closets and drawers	2 x Y
Straighten closets and drawers	M

OFFICE

Same routine as living room, plus:

Clean out all files	Y
Pay bills	W or M

MISCELLANEOUS

Laundry	2 x W
Water Plants	W
Check batteries in fire alarm	S
Salt in softener	M or as needed

GARAGE

Sweep out   E3M

Clean out car   M

Outside chores can be listed and put into your

routine as well.

Other things you can put on your calendar:

- Mending
- Ironing
- Cleaning out your purse
- Taking care of plants/gardening
- Pet care
- Cleaning the garage, basement, attic
- Working on scrapbooks or photo albums

The beauty of this system is that you don't have to do this all at once. You can spread this out over a year. Once you are organized and start to incorporate this into your weekly plan, it is very doable.

Your house will still look so much better with the new habits that you have established. It is much easier to do the underneath cleaning when your room is presentable already.

Storage

We all have things we need or want to keep. The best way to store and be able to find things when you need them is to have tubs or boxes and label them. If you have a space to keep them all in together, like a big closet or attic, that works great. It's important to mark each tub with a letter or number and write down what is in that tub and where it is located. You then need to either keep a master list on your computer or in a special notebook or 3x5 card in your recipe box. For example: *Christmas decorations: A —Christmas tree and skirt for bottom and lights for inside and out. B— Decorations for the tree and the fireplace.* This system can be used for all the things you want to store and will make things so easy to find when you need them. Another example would be clothes that you hand down to the next child. The time saved using a system like this is invaluable.

***

I understand there are seasons in life when all you can do are the basics. As long as you can get the laundry and the dishes done and run a vacuum once in a while and make the beds, the house will still be presentable. The nice thing is that when you are already organized you can get away with doing less for a time. Remember, it's not the way you plan but the doing of it that works.

ENCOURAGEMENT

At this point, you may be thinking, *Is this women nuts? My life and house are such a mess I will never get out of this. I can't possibly do all this*! Let me encourage you to look at it this way:

WHAT IF I ONLY….did my dishes every day?

WHAT IF I ONLY…got up earlier and got ready for the day before the majority of my family?

WHAT IF I ONLY... made my bed every day?

WHAT IF I ONLY...made a short schedule and tried to follow that?

WHAT IF I ONLY...read a few verses in the Bible and talked to God for a few minutes a day?

Maybe, just maybe, if you only did one of those things on a regular basis, could that make a difference in your life? You can do this—I know, because I have done it and I am still doing it.

All this change does not come immediately. Nothing worth having is quick and easy, but as the saying goes, how do you eat an elephant? One bite at a time. For you, it's one day at a time. One dish at a time. One bed at a time. This is doable.

There are dreams we all have. The writing of this book is an example. I let so many things stop me at different times. The negative voices in my head said I couldn't do this. But I knew that the people who really need this are like me. Why do we let opportunities pass us by? Don't let another day pass without doing one thing toward your goal. If you are eight or one hundred and eight, it is never too late.

We all know that there is no peace in disorganization. When the house is a wreck, bills are not paid because we don't even know where they are. The company from out of town is coming and everything is in a mess. How peaceful can that be? Our lives have to have some kind of structure or else they're just frustrating, and could even be harmful to our health.

As I've said before, you have to make the decision to get organized. No one else can make that decision for you! Though the answer is simple, it's so hard to put into practice. Make your plan and work your plan! Don't let anyone tell you that you can't do this. Consider all the things you have accomplished in your life; you had to overcome days when you didn't feel like it, but you kept pressing on. Often the hardest part is getting started, and once I have started, I become committed and am more likely to finish it.

Reading this book puts you at a crossroads. What do you want out of life? Are you willing to put in the time and effort to become organized? You can't expect to have the life you want without having some order in it. It's up to you!

LET ALL THINGS BE DONE DECENTLY AND IN ORDER.

1 CORINTHIANS 14:40

Now it's the time to answer the question. Does the washer really eat the socks? The short answer is no. The socks are under the bed or under the couch or out in the sandbox. They are everywhere they don't belong. It will be interesting to see where you find them as your organize your home. In fact, I would love to hear from you as you share all the places you find them. What an interesting list that would be! Email me at organizedhomemanagement@gmail.com If you are truly tired of living the way you are, there is a better way. It's one day at a time. It's one drawer and one closet at a time. It is not perfection but progress and it will change your life. So let's get going and remember starting is half done!

SIMPLE STEPS TO GET

ORGANIZED

GET A GOOD START ON EACH DAY

DO DAILY TASKS FIRST

TACKLE THE UNDERNEATH

 DO IT NOW

PICK IT UP, DON'T PASS IT UP

DON'T PILE—FILE

DIVIDE BIG JOBS INTO SMALL JOBS

ESTABLISH A FAMILY MESSAGE CENTER

A PLACE FOR EVERTHING AND

EVERTHING IN ITS PLACE

ORGANIZATION IS A HABIT, NOT

SOMETHING YOU DO SOMETIMES

MOTIVATION FOLLOWS ACTION

NOT BEING ORGANIZED IS TOO MUCH

WORK

STARTING IS HALF

DONE!!!

Acknowledgments

I want to thank my husband, Allen, and my children, Penny, Tom, Andy, and John. They have always encouraged me in my endeavors. A very special thank you to my daughter, Penny, for helping me many years ago to start this book. She also helped me teach some classes after she and I got organized. Another very special thank you to my niece Susie—without her encouragement this book would never have been finished. Thank you also to my second cousin Lila for her pre-editing ability. Also a special thank you to our computer tech Corey for his much needed help and Christy a former co-worker for her computer knowledge.

I have much to be thankful for. Most of all thank you, Jesus, for saving me and leading me to this knowledge and helping me to discipline myself and become a more organized homemaker for many years now. A special thank you to God for giving me God-fearing parents who also had a sense of humor. I am forever grateful for laughter.